HUGS
AWE SOME
XOXO
SMILE

Happy
Valentine's
Day!

HUGS
SMILE
AWE SOME
XOXO
I ♥ U
BESTIE
YOU ROCK
LOL
G.O.A.T.

BESTIE
G.O.A.T.
I ♥ U
HUGS
YOU ROCK
LOL
SMILE
AWE SOME
XOXO

What do you call a sheep dipped in chocolate?

A chocolate BAAAA!

Why did the donut give his sweetie a box of Valentine's candy?

Because he was DO-NUTS about her!

What did the car say to the panda bear?

You DRIVE me crazy!!

How do you talk to a big Valentine's Day Monster?

Use **BIG** words!

What kind of jokes do unicorns tell?

Uni-Corny ones!

Where do cows go on Valentine's Day?

To the MOOO-vies!

Why did the cats get married?

They were a PURR-fect match!

What do you do with a blue whale?

Cheer him up with a Valentine's card!

Knock, knock.
Who's there?
Dots.
Dots who?
Dots for me to know and you
to find out!

Why is the seahorse friends with the shark?

Because he is JAWSOME!

What do you call two birds in love?

TWEET-hearts!

What goes up when its raining cats and dogs?

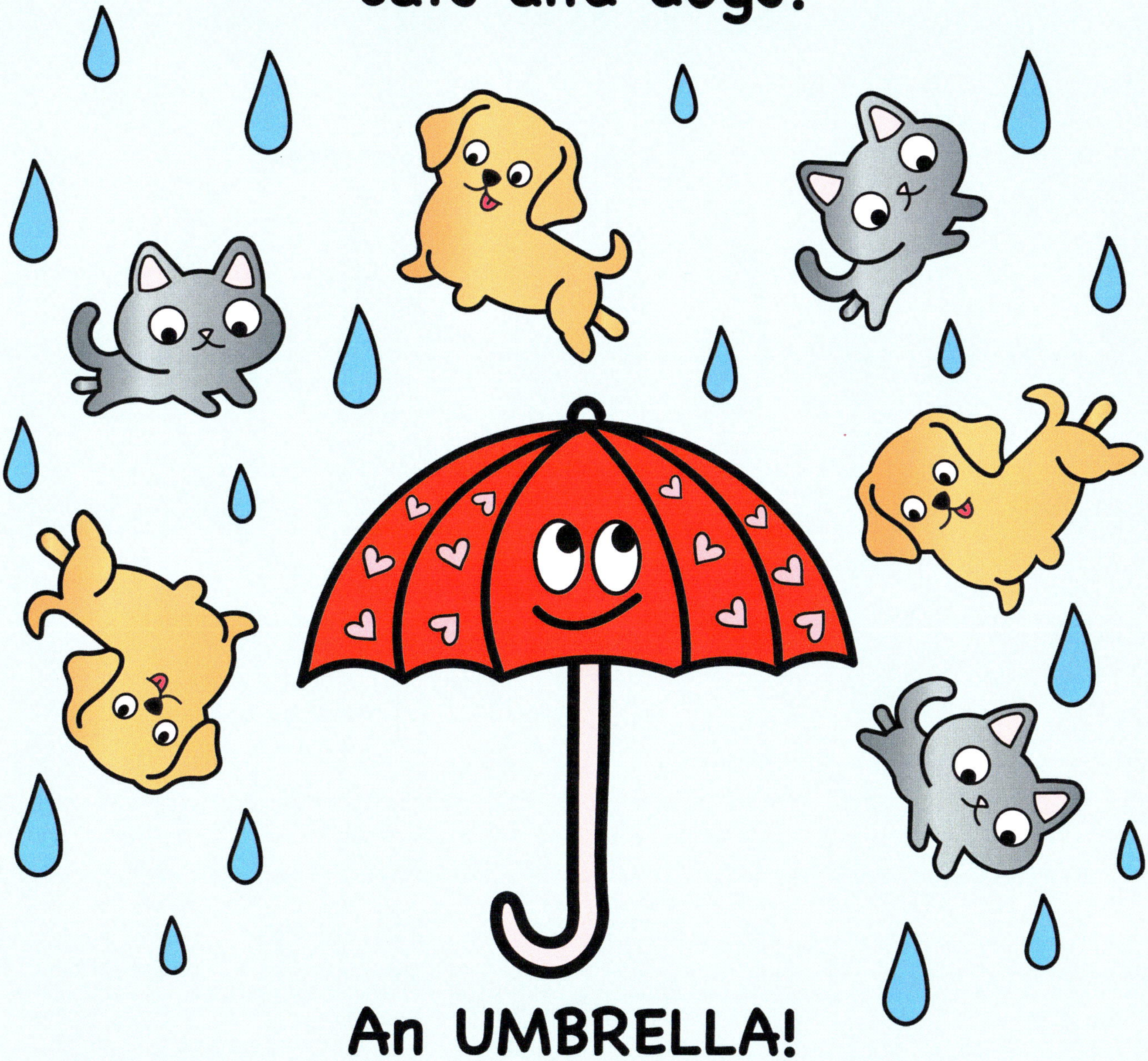

An UMBRELLA!

What did the dog say on Valentine's Day?

"WOOF you be my Valentine?"

What did the ghost say to his sweetie on Valentine's Day?

You are so BOOO-tiful!

Why should you invite a llama to a Valentine's Day party?

Because they are a LLAMA fun!

What day of the week does T. rex eat his Valentine's Day candy?

On CHEWS-day!

How do flowers kiss?

With their TULIPS!

Knock, knock.
Who's there?
Orange juice.
Orange juice who?
Orange juice glad it is
Valentine's Day!

What did the Valentine toothpick say to the heart-shaped sandwich?

You are full of BALONEY!

What did one volcano say to the other valcano?

I LAVA you!

What do you say to a pig on Valentine's Day?

I like you PIG time!

What did the snake give his girlfriend?

Hugs and HISSES!

What did the snail say to the other snail on Valentine's Day?

Will you be my Valen-SLIME?

Who sends out smelly Valentine's Day cards?

A STINKY-saurus!

What did one bee say to the other bee?

I like BEE-ing with you!

What did the shovel say to the sand castle?

I really DIG you!

Knock, knock.
Who's there?
Pizza.
Pizza who?
You have a PIZZA my heart!

Why did the kitty put Valentine candy under her pillow?

She wanted to have SWEET DREAMS!

What is an octopus's favorite song?

I want to hold your hand, hand, hand, hand, hand!

Knock, knock.
Who's there?
Some.
Some who?
Some BUNNY loves you!

HUGS
SMILE
AWE SOME
XOXO
I ♥ U
BESTIE
YOU ROCK
LOL
G.O.A.T.

BESTIE
G.O.A.T.
I ♥ U
HUGS
YOU ROCK
LOL
SMILE
AWE SOME
XOXO

Thanks for Spreading the Laughter
with these Cupid-Approved
Valentine Jokes!

Please consider leaving us a review on Amazon.com. We value your feedback & greatly appreciate your time!

Thank you
B. N. Silly

Made in the USA
Middletown, DE
11 February 2026

28389656R00022